values

Honesty

www.av2books.com

**Cynthia Amoroso
and Danielle Jacklin**

LET'S READ

AV²
BY WEIGL™

ADDED VALUE • AUDIO VISUAL

Go to **www.av2books.com**,
and enter this book's
unique code.

BOOK CODE

U 4 7 2 6 7 2

AV² by Weigl brings you media
enhanced books that support
active learning.

AV² provides enriched content that supplements and complements this book. Weigl's AV² books strive to create inspired learning and engage young minds in a total learning experience.

Your AV² Media Enhanced books come alive with...

 Audio
Listen to sections of
the book read aloud.

 Video
Watch informative
video clips.

 Embedded Weblinks
Gain additional information
for research.

 Try This!
Complete activities and
hands-on experiments.

 Key Words
Study vocabulary, and
complete a matching
word activity.

 Quizzes
Test your knowledge.

 Slide Show
View images and
captions, and prepare
a presentation.

... and much, much more!

Published by AV² by Weigl
350 5th Avenue, 59th Floor New York, NY 10118
Website: www.av2books.com

Project Coordinator: Danielle Jacklin
Art Director: Terry Paulhus

Library of Congress Control Number: 2017930866

ISBN 978-1-4896-6067-1 (hardcover)
ISBN 978-1-4896-6068-8 (softcover)
ISBN 978-1-4896-6069-5 (multi-user eBook)

Printed in the United States of America in Brainerd, Minnesota
1 2 3 4 5 6 7 8 9 0 21 20 19 18 17

032017
020317

Every reasonable effort has been made to trace ownership and to obtain permission to reprint copyright material. The publisher would be pleased to have any errors or omissions brought to its attention so that they may be corrected in subsequent printings.

The publisher acknowledges iStock, Getty, Alamy, and Shutterstock as the primary image suppliers for this title.

CONTENTS

What Is Honesty?

Have you ever told a lie? Have you ever tried to **cheat**? Everyone has times when they could lie or cheat. But honesty means telling the truth. It means not cheating. Honesty is not always easy. It takes strength. But it is the right thing to do. And it feels good!

Honesty feels better than cheating!

Honesty at School

Your teacher gives you homework. She tells you to do it over the weekend. You end up playing with friends. You forget all about your homework! On Monday, your teacher asks for the homework. You show honesty by telling the truth. You do not make **excuses**. You do not copy another student's work.

Sometimes telling the truth can be scary.

Money Mistakes

Maybe you like to go to the store after school. Your **favorite** gum costs 50 cents. You give the clerk one dollar. She should give you 50 cents back. But she gives you 75 cents by mistake. You know she gave you too much money. You show honesty by telling her she made a mistake. You give the extra money back.

Honesty means not taking more than your share.

Honesty and Cheating

You are playing a board game. You are unhappy because your friend is winning. He goes to the kitchen for a snack. You could move your piece farther ahead. Then you might win! But you show honesty by not cheating. You follow the rules—even if it means you will lose. Maybe you will win next time!

Knowing you have played honestly feels better than cheating.

Honesty and Waiting

The swirly slide is the best thing on the playground. Kids are lined up, waiting to use it. You are waiting your turn. The person in front of you looks the other way. There is room in front of her. She might not notice if you went ahead. You show honesty by waiting your turn.

Honesty means being fair about taking your turn.

Taking the Cake

Your dad has baked chocolate cake. He made it to take to a party. Chocolate cake is your favorite! It looks really good, and you are hungry. You eat a piece. Your mom sees that some is missing. She wants to know who ate it. You could **blame** your younger brother. But you show honesty by telling the truth.

Honesty means telling the truth, even if it will get you in trouble.

Honesty at Home

Your older brother has some money. He leaves it on the table. It would be easy to take it. You could put it in your piggy bank. He would not know where the money went. But you show honesty by leaving the money alone. You tell your brother where he left it.

Honesty means not taking things that belong to others.

Honesty and the Lost-and-Found

You and your friends are playing at the park. You see a bag near the swings. There are toys in the bag! Somebody has forgotten to take them home. You would love to have some of the toys. But you know they belong to someone else. You show honesty by taking them to the lost-and-found.

Honesty means returning things that are not yours.

Honesty is Important!

Honesty shows people that you tell the truth. It shows others that they can **trust** you. People want friends who are honest. They want family members who are honest, too. People will trust you when they know you tell the truth!

It is nice to be trusted!

Key Words

blame: When you blame someone, you say they have done something wrong.

cheat: When you cheat, you break the rules on purpose.

excuses: Excuses are reasons why you did not do something.

favorite: When you like something best, it is your favorite.

trust: When you know someone is honest, you can trust them.

Index

What You've Learned

Honesty feels better than cheating!

Knowing you have played honestly feels better than cheating.

Honesty means telling the truth, even if it will get you in trouble.

Sometimes telling the truth can be scary.

Honesty means being fair about taking your turn.

Honesty means returning things that are not yours.

Honesty means not taking more than your share.

Honesty means not taking things that belong to others.

It is nice to be trusted!